Felix Mendelssohn

COMPLETE SONGS WITHOUT WORDS

for Piano

DOVER PUBLICATIONS, INC.
Mineola, New York

Bibliographical Note

This Dover edition, first published in 2008, is excerpted from *Complete Works for Pianoforte Solo,* published in 1975 by Dover Publications, Inc., New York. This in turn was based on Series II of *Felix Mendelssohn Bartholdy's Werke. Kritisch durchgesehene Ausgabe von Julius Rietz. Mit Genehmigung der Originalverleger,* originally published by Breitkopf & Härtel, Leipzig, between 1874 and 1877.

International Standard Book Number
ISBN-13: 978-0-486-46614-9
ISBN-10: 0-486-46614-0

Manufactured in the United States by Courier Corporation
46614003   2015
www.doverpublications.com

CONTENTS

COMPLETE SONGS
WITHOUT WORDS

Six Songs Without Words (Book I), Op. 19

No. 4, composed 1829, is dedicated to Sophia Louisa Dance.
Original publisher: N. Simrock, Berlin.

Poco agitato.

Nº 5.

11

Venetianisches Gondellied (Venetian Gondola Song)

Six Songs Without Words (Book II), Op. 30

Dedicated to Elisa von Woringen. No. 4 composed 1834; No. 5 composed 1833.
Original publisher: N. Simrock, Berlin.

Allegro di molto.

Nº 2.

22

Andante grazioso.
Il Basso sempre piano e leggierissimo

No. 5.

24

Venetianisches Gondellied (Venetian Gondola Song)

Six Songs Without Words (Book III), Op. 38

Dedicated to Rosa von Woringen. No. 5 composed 1837; No. 6 composed 1836.
Original publisher: N. Simrock, Berlin.

Allegro non troppo.

Nº 2.

Presto e molto vivace.

Nº 3.

34

Duetto.

N.B.: Both voices should be equally prominent and clear throughout.

Six Songs Without Words (Book IV), Op. 53

Dedicated to Sophie Horsley. Nos. 5 and 6 composed 1841.
Original publisher: N. Simrock, Berlin.

Volkslied (Folk Song)

Allegro con fuoco.

Nº 5.

Six Songs Without Words (Book V), Op. 62

Dedicated to Clara Schumann. No. 1 composed 1844; No. 2 composed 1843; No. 6 composed 1842.
Original publisher: N. Simrock, Berlin.

Allegro con fuoco.

Nº 2.

61

Venetianisches Gondellied (Venetian Gondola Song)

Six Songs Without Words (Book VI), Op. 67

Dedicated to Sophie Rosen. No. 1 composed 1843; No. 2 composed 1845; No. 5 composed 1844.
Original publisher: N. Simrock, Berlin.

Andante tranquillo.

No. 3.

Six Songs Without Words (Book VII), Op. 85

No. 2 composed 1834; Nos. 4 and 5 composed 1845; No. 6 composed 1841.
Original publisher: N. Simrock, Berlin.

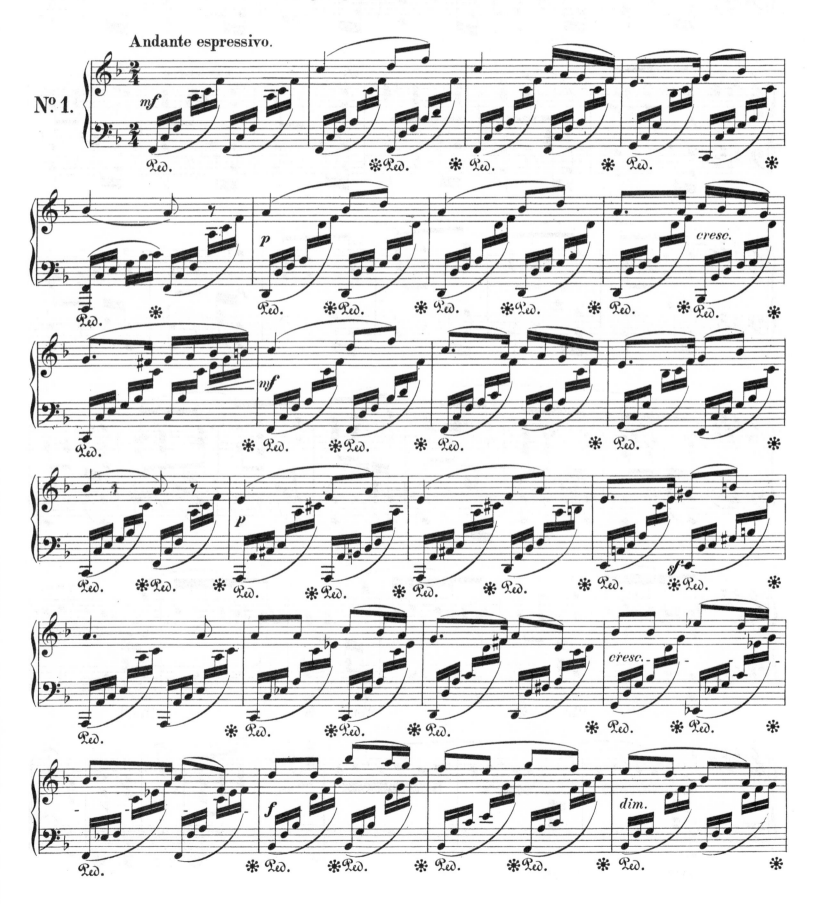

85

Allegro agitato.

N.º 2.

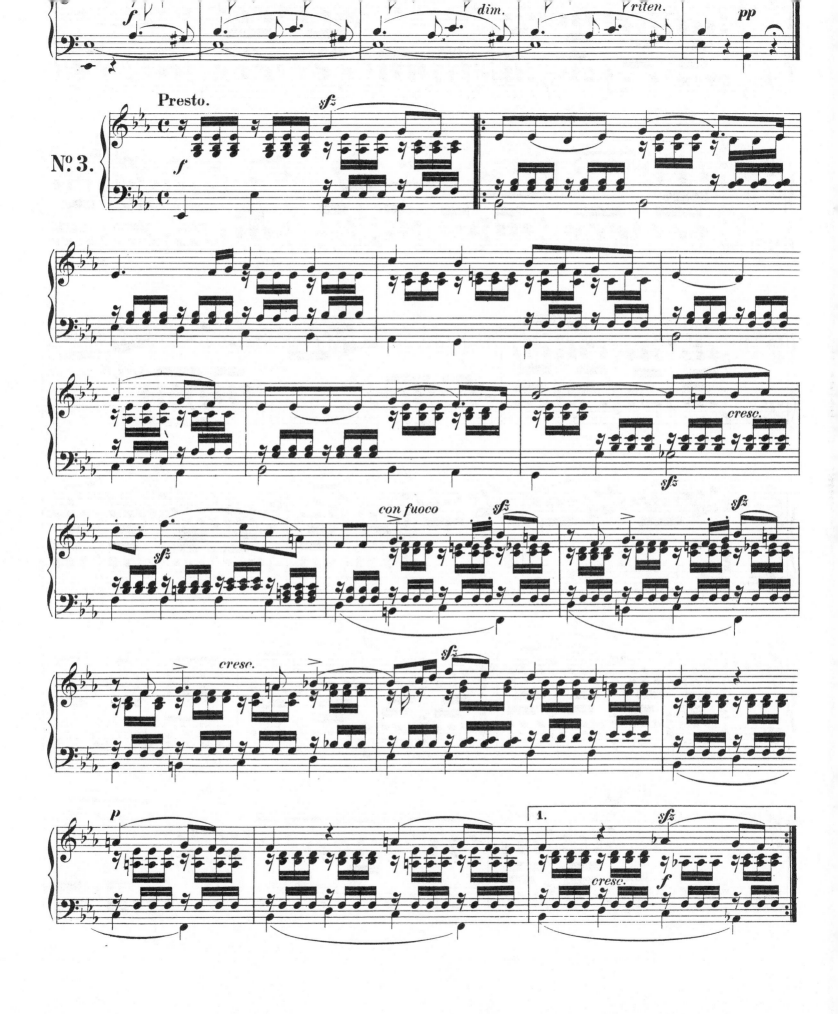

N.º 6.

Allegretto con moto.

sempre cantabile

p sempre stacc.

Six Songs Without Words (Book VIII), Op. 102

No. 1 composed 1842; Nos. 2, 3 and 5 composed 1845.
Original publisher: N. Simrock, Berlin.